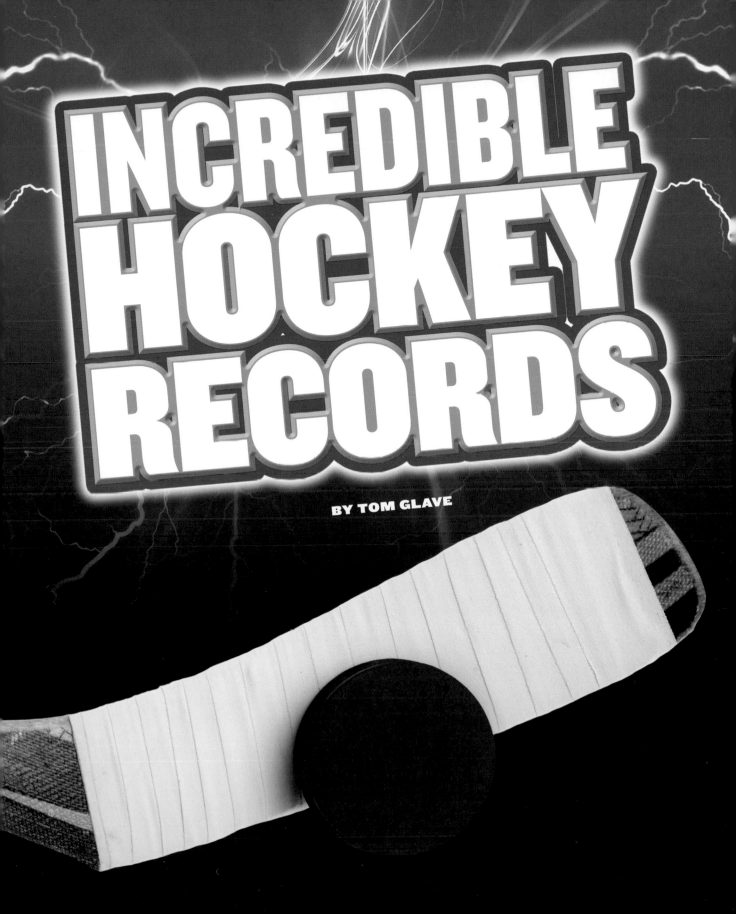

INCREDIBLE HOCKEY RECORDS

BY TOM GLAVE

Published by The Child's World®
1980 Lookout Drive • Mankato, MN 56003-1705
800-599-READ • www.childsworld.com

Acknowledgments
The Child's World®: Mary Swensen, Publishing Director
Red Line Editorial: Editorial direction and production
The Design Lab: Design

Photographs ©: Dan Kosmayer/Shutterstock Images, cover, 1, 2, 23; Dino Vournas/
AP Images, 5; Bettmann/Corbis, 6, 9, 10, 13, 14, 19; Rusty Kennedy/AP Images, 16;
J. C. Anderson/Bettmann/Corbis, 20; Alan Diaz/AP Images, 21

Design Elements: Shutterstock Images

ISBN 9781503808898
LCCN 2015958450

Printed in the United States of America
Mankato, MN
June, 2016
PA02307

TABLE OF CONTENTS

CHAPTER 1

GOALIE RECORDS

MOST REGULAR-SEASON VICTORIES
691 Victories
Martin Brodeur, 1992–2015

Martin Brodeur helped the New Jersey Devils win a lot of games. He also led them to three Stanley Cup championships. He set the National Hockey League (NHL) record for regular-season wins by a goalie in 2009. The old record of 551 was set by longtime Montreal Canadiens great Patrick Roy.

Brodeur won 688 games in 21 years with New Jersey. He added three wins with St. Louis before retiring in 2015. Brodeur also set NHL records with 125 regular-season **shutouts** and 24 in the **playoffs**.

MOST CONSECUTIVE SHUTOUTS
5 Shutouts
Brian Boucher, Phoenix Coyotes

Keeping a team from scoring for an entire game is hard. Doing it in back-to-back games is almost impossible. But Brian Boucher of the Phoenix Coyotes went five games without allowing a goal.

His streak started on New Year's Eve 2003, when he shut down the Los Angeles Kings at home. Then the Coyotes went on a four-game road trip. Boucher was flawless. He blanked the Dallas Stars, Carolina Hurricanes, Washington Capitals, and Minnesota Wild. No modern-era goalie has matched that streak. Alex Connell of the Ottawa Senators had six straight shutouts in 1928. But many NHL rules have changed to make scoring easier since then.

BRIAN BOUCHER

GLENN HALL

MOST CONSECUTIVE COMPLETE GAMES

502 Games

Glenn Hall, 1955–1962

Glenn Hall didn't miss a game for seven consecutive seasons. Not only that, he played every minute in goal for 502 games. Hall's streak started in 1955 when he played for the Detroit Red Wings. After two years, the Red Wings traded Hall to Chicago. The streak continued for five more years. The player nicknamed "Mr. Goalie" helped the Blackhawks win the Stanley Cup in 1961. Hall finally missed a game in November 1962 due to a back injury.

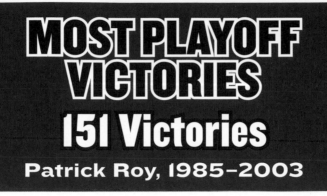

MOST PLAYOFF VICTORIES

151 Victories

Patrick Roy, 1985–2003

Patrick Roy was at his best when his team needed it the most. Roy won four Stanley Cups and a record 151 playoff games. Roy helped Montreal win the Stanley Cup as a **rookie**. He won 11 straight playoff games in 1993 as the Canadiens won another cup. Then he led the Colorado Avalanche to championships in 1996 and 2001.

SMITH STONEWALLS MONTREAL

Detroit goalie Normie Smith once stopped 92 shots in a single game. It was a playoff game in 1936 against the Montreal Maroons. The Red Wings scored in the sixth **overtime** to win 1–0. Smith blanked the Maroons for 176 minutes and 30 seconds in the NHL's longest game.

CHAPTER 2

GRETZKY RECORDS

MOST GOALS IN A SEASON
92 Goals
1981–82

Wayne Gretzky did a lot of amazing things on the ice. He holds more records than anyone in NHL history. His most famous feat might be breaking the single-season goals record. Gretzky started the 1981–82 season hot. He scored 50 goals in Edmonton's first 39 games. He had five goals in one game to reach 50. He broke Phil Esposito's record of 76 goals on February 24, 1982. He scored three times against the Buffalo Sabres in that game. That was one of his 10 **hat tricks** that season.

Alexander Ovechkin scored 65 goals in 2007–08. That's the closest any current player has come to the record.

LONGEST POINT STREAK
51 Games
1983–84

Hockey players get a point for a goal or an **assist**. In 1983–84, Gretzky had at least one point during the Oilers' first 51 games. Gretzky scored 61 goals and had 92 assists during the streak. He recorded eight points in a game twice during the streak.

The streak was almost stopped twice. He scored with two seconds left in the 44th game. He later played four games with an injured shoulder, but he still kept the streak alive. The Los Angeles Kings finally kept him off the score sheet on January 28, 1984.

WAYNE GRETZKY

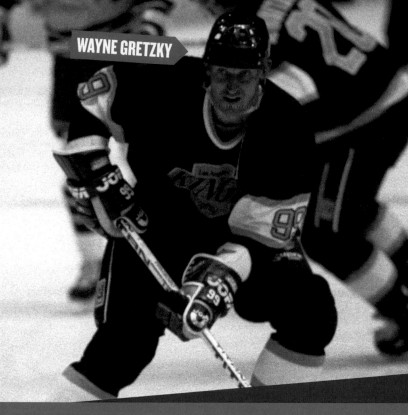

MOST POINTS IN A SEASON
215 Points
1985–86

The 1985–86 season was one of Gretzky's best. He set the NHL record with 163 assists. He also scored 52 goals. He had a part in 215 of Edmonton's 426 goals that season. Gretzky broke his own single-season record of 212 points. He had three assists on April 4, 1986, to break his old record. He added an assist in the next game for his 215th point. Gretzky is the only NHL player to score 200 points in a season. He did it four times!

MOST CAREER POINTS
2,857 Points
1978–1999

Gretzky is the NHL's all-time leader with 894 goals and 1,963 assists. He is the only player to accumulate more than 2,000 career points. The next-closest player is his longtime teammate Mark Messier, who finished his career with 1,887 points. Gretzky broke Gordie Howe's record of 1,850 points on October 15, 1989. Gretzky had two goals and an assist for the Los Angeles Kings that night.

A GREAT NICKNAME

Gretzky is nicknamed "The Great One." He played in the NHL for 20 years. He holds more than 60 NHL records. He was named the NHL's Most Valuable Player (MVP) nine times. He was the scoring champion 10 times. Those are both records. The NHL retired his jersey in 2000. No player from any team will ever wear No. 99 again.

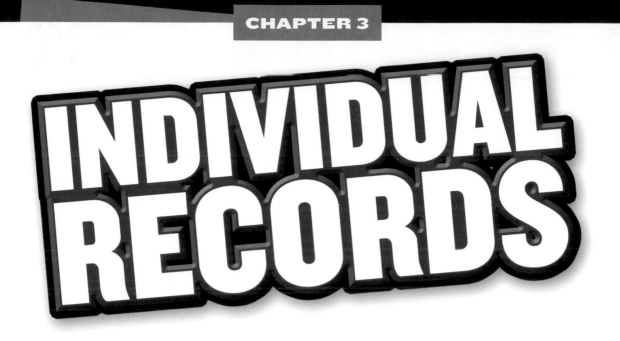

CHAPTER 3

INDIVIDUAL RECORDS

MOST GOALS BY A ROOKIE
76 Goals
Teemu Selanne, 1992–93

Teemu Selanne broke into the NHL with a bang. The Winnipeg Jets star had a hat trick in his fifth game. And he didn't stop there. Selanne scored four goals in a late February game. That gave him 51. He scored a hat trick in the Jets' next game, too. That broke Mike Bossy's rookie record of 53 goals. Selanne finished with 76 goals. His 132 points were another rookie record.

FASTEST HAT TRICK
21 Seconds
Bill Mosienko, Chicago Blackhawks
March 23, 1952

Bill Mosienko scored 258 goals in his 14-year career with the Chicago Blackhawks. He is probably best known for the three goals he scored in 21 seconds against the New York Rangers. Mosienko scored off an assist from Gus Bodnar 6:09 into the third period. Bodnar won the next two faceoffs. His passes found Mosienko. The last goal was scored at 6:30 of the third period. Amazingly, Bodnar won the next faceoff and Mosienko had another chance to score seven seconds later. But his shot hit the goalpost. Chicago won the game 7–6.

BILL MOSIENKO

13

GORDIE HOWE

MOST CAREER GAMES
1,767 Games
Gordie Howe, 1946–1980

Gordie Howe is called "Mr. Hockey" for a good reason. Howe played for the Detroit Red Wings for 25 seasons. He led the NHL in scoring six times. He also was the league MVP six times. Detroit won four Stanley Cups with Howe leading the way.

Mr. Hockey retired in 1971. But two years later he joined the upstart World Hockey Association (WHA). He played there for six years. When the WHA folded, Howe played one more NHL season with the Hartford Whalers. He was 52 years old. Howe retired again in 1980.

MOST GOALS IN A GAME
7 Goals
Joe Malone, Quebec Bulldogs
January 31, 1920

Joe Malone was one of the NHL's first scoring stars. The NHL was in its third year in 1920. The Quebec Bulldogs played host to the Toronto St. Patricks. Malone scored one goal in the first period. He had a hat trick in the second period and two **shorthanded** goals in the third period. He added the seventh goal late in the game. The Bulldogs won 10–6.

HOCKEY
AT THE BIG HOUSE

The University of Michigan's football stadium hosted the 2014 NHL Winter Classic. The NHL sold 105,491 tickets for the outdoor game between Detroit and Toronto. It broke the previous NHL attendance record of 71,217.

DAVE SCHULTZ

MOST PENALTY MINUTES IN A SEASON
472 Penalty Minutes
Dave Schultz, Philadelphia Flyers
1974–75

Dave "The Hammer" Schultz was the leader of a crew known as "The Broad Street Bullies." The Philadelphia Flyers were known as a physical team. Schultz got into a lot of fights. He got kicked out of a lot of games. Those **penalties** added up fast. Schultz set an NHL record with 348 penalty minutes during the 1973–74 season. He shattered that record the next year. But The Hammer was a big part of the Flyers' success. Philadelphia won the Stanley Cup both seasons.

MOST POINTS IN A GAME
10 Points
Darryl Sittler, Toronto Maple Leafs
February 7, 1976

Darryl Sittler scored six goals in one game. That was not an NHL record. However, he also had four assists in that game. That gave him a record 10 points. Sittler had two assists in the first period against the Boston Bruins. He added three goals and two assists in the second period. Then Sittler scored three more times in the third period. Toronto won 11–4.

OFFENSIVE DEFENSEMEN

Sometimes a **defenseman** gets involved with the offense. Bobby Orr set two NHL records with the Boston Bruins during the 1970–71 season. He had the most points (139) and assists (102) by a defenseman in one season. Paul Coffey holds the record for most goals by a defenseman. He scored 48 goals for the Edmonton Oilers in 1985–86.

CHAPTER 4

TEAM RECORDS

MOST STANLEY CUPS
24 Stanley Cups
Montreal Canadiens

The Canadiens have been around longer than the NHL. The team started playing in 1909. It won the Stanley Cup in 1916. It joined the new NHL the next year. Montreal won a record five straight Stanley Cups between 1956 and 1960. There were only six teams in the NHL then. The Canadiens added four straight championships between 1976 and 1979. Toronto is second with 13 Stanley Cups.

CONSECUTIVE PLAYOFF SERIES VICTORIES

19 Series

New York Islanders, 1980–1984

Beginning in 1980, NHL teams had to win four series to win the Stanley Cup. That year the New York Islanders started a streak of four straight Stanley Cup championships. That meant the Islanders won 16 straight playoff series between 1980 and 1983. Then they won their first three playoff series in 1984. They reached the Stanley Cup Final again but lost to the Edmonton Oilers, ending their streak at 19.

MARIO LEMIEUX

LONGEST WINNING STREAK
17 Games
Pittsburgh Penguins, 1992–93

Pittsburgh went on a hot streak late in the 1992–93 season. Star center Mario Lemieux returned to the lineup in early March after missing two months due to an illness. Soon the Penguins were unstoppable. Lemieux scored 27 goals and had 24 assists during their record run. The streak finally ended with a tie at New Jersey in the final game of the season.

The Philadelphia Flyers once went 35 games without a loss. They had a streak of 25 wins and 10 ties during the 1979–80 season. The NHL now uses shootouts to break ties.

LONGEST SHOOTOUT
20 Rounds
Washington Capitals at Florida Panthers
December 16, 2014

The NHL started using shootouts to break ties in 2005. Three players from each team take turns shooting at the goalie. If they're still tied after three rounds, they continue one round at a time until one team scores and the other does not.

The Capitals and Panthers had a history-making shootout in 2014. The teams were tied 1–1 at the end of **regulation**. Washington scored five times in the shootout, but each time the Panthers extended the game with a goal on their turn. Finally, in the 20th round, Panthers goalie Roberto Luongo stopped Alex Ovechkin. Then Nick Bjugstad beat Capitals goalie Braden Holtby to win the game for Florida.

BRADEN HOLTBY

assist (uh-SISST): An assist is a pass or shot that leads to a teammate's goal. Bill Mosienko scored off Gus Bodnar's assist three times in a row.

defenseman (di-FENSS-muhn): A defenseman is a skater whose main job is to keep the opponent from scoring. Bobby Orr was a defenseman who also scored a lot.

hat tricks (HAT TRIKS): Hat tricks occur when one player scores three goals in a game. Wayne Gretzky had 50 career hat tricks.

overtime (OH-vur-time): A game goes into overtime when the score is tied after three periods. Detroit beat the Montreal Maroons in the sixth overtime period.

penalties (PEN-uhl-teez): Penalties are punishment for breaking the rules. Dave Schultz committed a lot of penalties in his career.

playoffs (PLAY-awfs): The playoffs are a tournament played after the regular season to determine a champion. Patrick Roy played his best in the playoffs.

regulation (reg-yuh-LAY-shuhn): Regulation is the length of a normal game—three periods in hockey. The Capitals and Panthers were tied at the end of regulation.

rookie (ROOK-ee): A rookie is a first-year player. Teemu Selanne scored more goals than any other NHL rookie.

shorthanded (short-HAN-did): A team is shorthanded when it plays with fewer players than its opponent. Joe Malone scored twice while the Bulldogs were shorthanded.

shutouts (SHUT-owts): Shutouts are games in which one team fails to score. Brian Boucher recorded five shutouts in a row.

IN THE LIBRARY

Filipek, Steele. *Hockey Hotshots: Young Stars of the NHL*. New York: Grosset & Dunlap, 2010.

Herman, Gail, and Ted Hammond. *Who Is Wayne Gretzky?* New York: Grosset & Dunlap, 2015.

Jordan, Christopher. *We Are the Goalies: The Top Netminders of the NHL*. Plattsburgh, NY: Fenn/Tundra, 2013.

ON THE WEB

Visit our Web site for links about hockey: **childsworld.com/links**

Note to Parents, Teachers, and Librarians: We routinely verify our Web links to make sure they are safe and active sites. So encourage your readers to check them out!

INDEX

3 1333 04504 4482

ABOUT THE AUTHOR

Tom Glave learned to write about sports at the University of Missouri. He has covered sports for newspapers in New Jersey, Missouri, Arkansas, and Texas. He has also written several books about sports.